TROIS DUOS CONCERT

FOR TWO OBOES OR TWO SAXOPHONES.

W. FERLING.

Op 13.

OBOE 2.

SOUTHERN MUSIC COMPANY

RONDO.

DUO
No. 2.

Poco Adagio.

RONDO.

OBOE 2.

DUO
No. 3.

Allegro

Andante

RONDO-MINUETTO.
Poco vivace.

TRIO

for Two Oboes and English Horn
Op. 87

2nd Oboe

Ludwig van Beethoven
Revised by Albert J. Andraud

2nd Oboe

Adagio ♪=84
Cantabile

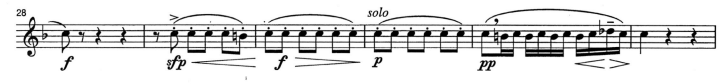

Ludwig van Beethoven

Op. 87

TRIO

for Two Oboes and English Horn

Revised by
Albert J. Andraud

Program Notes

Scholars disagree as to the specific dates of composition for Beethoven's Trio for Two Oboes and English Horn, Op. 87, but the work was first performed on a concert of the Vienna *Tonkünstler-Sozietät* on December 23, 1793. The rather interesting combination of two oboes and English horn is thought to have been suggested by a work by Johann Wendt for similar combination of instruments, and in any event, Beethoven admired the sound sufficiently to compose (in 1796-97) a set of variations on "La ci darem la mano" from Mozart's opera *Don Giovanni* for the same combination. The Trio, Op. 87 did not appear in print until 1806 (at which time the late opus number was applied) and not in the original form but in arrangements for two flutes/viola and two oboes/bassoon. The work has long been one of the composer's most popular works, appearing in dozens of editions for a wide variety of instruments, and although the music works very well in combinations of contrasting instruments, the true beauty of Beethoven's sonorities is heard in ensembles of instruments of like timbre. From a compositional standpoint, the piece lacks the depth of passion found in Beethoven's mature romantic works, but it bears all the charm and energy of his earlier, classically influenced scores, while clearly pointing the direction his composition would take.

About the Editor

Albert J. Andraud served as oboist and English horn soloist with the Cincinnati Symphony Orchestra for more than 25 years. A native of France, he served in the French army in World War I and, in 1918, came to the United States with the army band. He emigrated to the United States in 1921, playing oboe with the Chicago opera and the Cleveland Symphony before joining the Cincinnati Symphony in 1929. A man of immense self confidence, he was embroiled in a dispute with the conductor of the Cincinnati Symphony at the time of his retirement in April of 1955, and prior to the intermission of his final concert took an uninvited solo bow while the conductor "stood in icy immobility". Albert J. Andraud died in 1976 at the age of 91.

Mssr. Andraud's edition of Beethoven's Trio, Op. 87 expresses the French romantic tradition which was his heritage. Though some modern performers may take issue with some of the mannerisms found in this edition, the ready availability of the original Beethoven score will allow performers to discard any markings which might be questionable. Other performers may well enjoy a thoroughly romantic approach to this charming work.

SOUTHERN MUSIC COMPANY

TRIO
for Two Oboes and English Horn
Op. 87

English Horn

Ludwig van Beethoven
Revised by Albert J. Andraud

Lower notes are Beethoven's original writing.

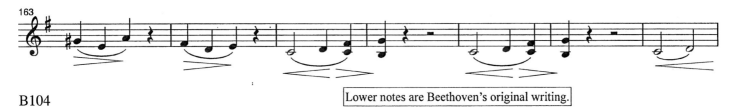

Lower notes are Beethoven's original writing.

B104

Menuetto da capo, senza replica e poi la Coda

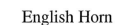

Large notes are Beethoven's original writing.

SELECTED SOLOS AND STUDIES FOR OBOE OR ENGLISH HORN

Oboe Etudes and Instruction

ANDRAUD, ALBERT J.
| B100 | Practical And Progressive Oboe Method | HL3770170 |

Long considered the "bible" for oboists, this comprehensive coil-bound volume begins with preliminary exercises for beginners and progresses through to the intermediate advanced level by the use of original studies and etudes by Albert Andraud, as well as classic melodies by the great composers and American folk song. Major and minor keys are introduced throughout, with a complete set of scale studies at the end of the book. Also included are a history of the instrument, the basics of tone production, lessons on ornamentation, and instructions for beginning reed making. Six complete solo works are also included in this exceptional volume:

BARRETT, APOLLON
Hite, David
| B383 | 40 Progressive Melodies | HL3770582 |

HAINES, HARRY
B329OB	Division Of Beat, Bk. 2	HL3770486
B497OB	Rhythm Master, Beginning Bk. 1	HL3770814
B502OB	Rhythm Master, Intermediate Bk 2	HL3770836

HAINES, HARRY
Rhodes, Tom
| B323OB | Division Of Beat, Bk. 1a | HL3770461 |

HITE, DAVID
Hite, David
| B380 | Melodious And Progressive Studies, Bk. 1 | HL3770579 |
| B473 | Melodious And Progressive Studies, Bk. 2 | HL3770716 |

VICTOR/ BIERSCHENK
Victor, John
| B354OB | Symphonic Band Technique | HL3770531 |

Oboe Solo with Keyboard

ANDRAUD, ALBERT J.
Andraud, Albert
| B107CO | 15 Grands Solos De Concert | HL3770181 |

A significant repertoire collection for the advancing oboe player/student. Includes works by: Mozart, Dallier, Bertain, Guihaud, Busser, Paladilhe, Neilsen, Colin, Lefebvre and J.S. Bach.

| B106CO | Oboist's Concert Album | HL3770178 |

BACH, J.S.
Andraud, Albert
| SS514 | Menuet And Famous Aria | HL3774147 |
| SS516 | Siciliano And Arioso | HL3774149 |

BAERMANN, CARL
Hite, David
| B495 | Foundation Studies | HL3770806 |

BARNES, JAMES
| ST578 | Autumn Soliloquy for Oboe | HL3775314 |
| Grade 3 |

BELLINI, VINCENZO
Harry Peters
| SS934 | Concerto In E Flat | HL3774621 |

COLIN, CHARLES
Andraud, Albert
| SS511 | Third Solo De Concert | HL3774144 |

DVORAK, ANTONIN
Prodan, James
| SU295 | Sonatina | HL3776178 |

EWAZEN, ERIC
| SU434 | Down A River of Time | HL3776351 |

A 3-movement concerto for oboe and string orchestra, Down A River of Time is an alternately joyous and wistful contemplation reflecting on life, memory, and the importance of dreams and ideals. Dedicated to oboist Linda Strommen who premiered the work with the American Sinfonietta. Duration ca. 23'.

GUILHAUD, GEORGES
Andraud, Albert
| SS505 | First Concertino | HL3774137 |

HANDEL, GEORGE FRIDERIC
Andraud, Albert
| SS182 | Concerto Grosso No. 8 In B Flat | HL3773789 |
| B108 | Five Solos | HL3770183 |

KREISLER, ALEXANDER VON
| SS695 | Sonatina | HL3774349 |

LENOM, CLEMENT
| SS261 | Musette | HL3773880 |

MOZART, WOLFGANG AMADEUS
Andraud, Albert
| SS504 | Concerto In E Flat, K294 | HL3774136 |

MOZART, WOLFGANG AMADEUS
Blair, Richard
| ST787 | Concerto In C, K314 | HL3775610 |

MOZART, WOLFGANG AMADEUS
Yvonne Desportes/ Albert Andraud
| SS153 | Concertino, K370 | HL3773758 |

NIELSEN, CARL
| SS510 | Romance And Humoresque | HL3774143 |

PIERNE, GABRIEL
Andraud, Albert
| ST219 | Piece In G Minor | HL3774830 |

ROSETTI, ANTONIO
Ronald Richards
| ST252 | Concerto In C | HL3774872 |
| ST251 | Concerto In D | HL3774871 |

TCHAIKOVSKY, PETER
Myron Zakopets
| SU278 | Romance | HL3776153 |

TELEMANN, GEORG PHILLIPP
Andraud, Albert
SS263	Concerto In F Minor	HL3773882
SS136	Sonata In A Minor	HL3773739
SS137	Sonata In G Minor	HL3773740

TELEMANN, GEORG PHILLIPP
Chidester, L.W.
| ST131 | Andante And Presto | HL3774717 |

English Horn Etudes and Instruction

ANDRAUD, ALBERT J.
| B412 | Vade Mecum Of The Oboist (230 Selected Technical and Orchestral Studies for Oboe and English horn) | HL3770621 |

(230 selected technical and orchestral studies for the Oboe or English Horn). Compiled and edited by Albert Andraud.

English Horn Solo with Keyboard

BOZZA, EUGENE
| SS268 | Divertissement | HL3773887 |

HANDEL, GEORGE FRIDERIC
Pezzi/ Albert Andraud
| SS133 | Concerto In C Minor | HL3773736 |

MOZART, WOLFGANG AMADEUS
Andraud, Albert
| SS272 | Adagio Religioso from Concerto, K622 | HL3773892 |

2nd Oboe

B104

10 DUETS

For 2 Oboes or 2 Saxophones

Aria

B. Bernards

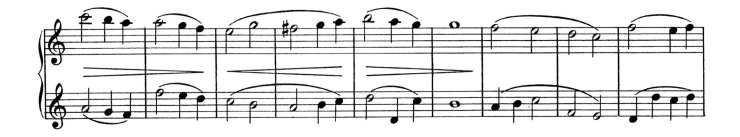

Canzonetta

N.º 2 Andante con moto

Romanze

Arietta

Longing

Nº 5 **Larghetto**

Joyful Hope

Nº 6 Valse

Lullaby

Nº 7 Lento

dim. e rallent.

In Confidence

Nº 8 Allegro moderato

Jazz-Etude

№ 9 Tempo di Foxtrot

D.C. al Fine

Thema und Variationen

Thema

Nº 10 Andante

Var. I

Var. II
Più lento

Var. III

Var. IV

Selected Oboe Publications

METHODS

ANDRAUD, ALBERT J.

B100   Practical and Progressive Oboe Method   HL3770170

Long considered the "bible" for oboists, this comprehensive coil-bound volume begins with preliminary exercises for beginners and progresses through to the intermediate advanced level by the use of original studies and etudes by Albert Andraud, as well as classic melodies by the great composers and American folk song. Major and minor keys are introduced throughout, with a complete set of scale studies at the end of the book. Also included are a history of the instrument, the basics of tone production, lessons on ornamentation, and instructions for beginning reed making. Six complete solo works are also included in this exceptional volume:

B412   Vade Mecum of the Oboist   HL3770621

230 selected technical and orchestral studies for the Oboe or English Horn). Compiled and edited by Albert Andraud.

BAERMANN, CARL

Hite, David

B495   Foundation Studies   HL3770806

Scales, chord and intervals for daily practice patterned after Carl Baermann, Op. 63.

FERLING, WILHELM

Andraud, Albert J.

B571   18 Studies, Op. 12   HL3770916

B103   48 Famous Studies, 1st Part   HL3770173

These studies have been long established as one of the centerpieces of study repertoire for both the oboe and saxophone.In addition to the 48 famous Ferling studies in includes 3 Duos Concertants for two instruments and Trio for two oboes and English horn by Beethoven. Second oboe/sax part available as 03770175.

B104   48 Famous Studies, 2nd Part   HL3770175

These studies have been long established as one of the centerpieces of study repertoire for both the oboe and saxophone. In addition to the 48 famous Ferling studies in includes 3 Duos Concertants for two instruments and Trio for two oboes and English horn by Beethoven. This is the 2nd part in the series.

HITE, DAVID

Hite, David

B383   40 Progressive Melodies   HL3770582

B380   Melodious and Progressive Studies, Bk. 1   HL3770579

Without question one of the finest oboe study collections ever published. Compiled and edited by master teacher David Hite. Includes: 36 Expressive Studies-Demnitz; 24 Melodic Studies-Nocentini; 24 Melodic Etudes-Baermann; Scales and Thirds-Klose.

COLLECTIONS

ANDRAUD, ALBERT J.

Andraud, Albert J.

B107   15 Grands Solos De Concert   HL3770181

A significant repertoire collection for the advancing oboe player/student. Includes works by: Mozart, Dallier, Bertain, Guihaud, Busser, Paladilhe, Neilsen, Colin, Lefebvre and J.S. Bach.

B106   Oboist's Concert Album: Contest Collection   HL3770178

A collection of 33 original oboe solos for contests and concerts, suitable for oboe or saxophone. Includes works by Bach, LeClair, Godard, Handel, Mozart, Pierne, and others.

HANDEL, GEORGE FRIDERIC

Andraud, Albert J.

B108   Five Solos   HL3770183

I. Famous Largo
II. Concerto in G Minor
III. Sonate I
IV. Sonate II
V. Sonate III

SOLO, UNACCOMPANIED

TELEMANN, GEORG PHILLIPP

Forrest, Sidney

B453   Fantasies I-xii (1 - 12)   HL3770644

SOLO WITH PIANO

BELLINI, VINCENZO

Peters, Harry

SS934   Concerto in E Flat   HL3774621

Edited by Harry Peters

EWAZEN, ERIC

SU434   Down a River of Time (reduction)   HL3776351

A 3-movement concerto for oboe and string orchestra, Down a River of Time is an alternately joyous and wistful contemplation reflecting on life, memory, and the importance of dreams and ideals. Dedicated to oboist Linda Strommen who premiered the work with the American Sinfonietta. Duration ca. 23'.

HANDEL, GEORGE FRIDERIC

Andraud, Albert J.

SS182   Concerto Grosso No. 8 in B Flat   HL3773789

MARCELLO, BENEDETTO

SS181   Concerto in c Minor   HL3773788

TELEMANN, GEORG PHILLIPP

Andraud, Albert J.

SS263   Concerto in f Minor   HL3773882

SS136   Sonata in a Minor   HL3773739

A four movement sonata, this piece offers the player the opportunity to play in the Baroque style with ornamentations. Movement titles: I. Siciliana: Andante grazioso
II. Spirituoso: Allegretto
III. Andante amabile
IV. Vivace

Exclusively distributed by **HAL•LEONARD® CORPORATION**

Questions/ comments? info@laurenkeisermusic.com